LIFE
After
DIVORCE

LIFE
After
DIVORCE

"In the aftermath of divorce,
you are the constructor of your own
happiness and freedom."

The following men are the contributing authors to this book and the Life *After* Divorce journey:

Carlon Manual

Clint Richardson

DaVon Robateau

DeAndre Weir

Donald Cherry

Floyd J. Sanders

Ivan T. Allen

Scott Looney

Tyrone Auston

Vince Plair

Contents

The Vision and the Movement

What is a vision and what is a movement? In short, a *vision* is seeing something before you see it. A *movement* brings a group of people together with common interest about a certain thing that they all want to see change for the better, bringing awareness to it, and giving support, and ideas about how to reach the goal.

The Life *After* Divorce movement was born in 2021 when Tamora K. Burton, affectionately known as Tam, invited other women who had the same experiences, to share their story but mainly give hope to others going through divorce, as co-authors in the first anthology *Life After Divorce*. The movement includes discussion of how healing during and after a divorce can help mend the scars, fix the brokenness, and catapult the person experiencing divorce to the starting point of healing or for some maintaining healing that they have done through the work in their process. The growth of the movement now includes men who have experienced divorce and are willing to share the healing journey.

Tam has a very unique way of describing her vision. She decided to continue to curate it by getting a few men who have experienced divorce and the process of healing. In Tam's description of her vision, (healing by removing one layer of pain at a time) she deems it important that we know the process of healing is not done overnight nor is there a timeline on the process. However, giving yourself permission to remove the layers is what you must commit to.

Committing to removing layers can be a challenge because most of it will require you to tap back into your remembrance of the "why to the what." Please do not let that detour you from continuing to flip the pages of this book. Instead, let it encourage you and prepare your mind to shift into the stage of removing layers of pain. Be ready to read from the point of view of other men who have worked the process and are now able to share the tools that they used.

The co-authors of this project are hoping that they could be for you what they once needed while in the (divorce) shoes themselves. Tam's vision is for each divorcee to remove the layers of the experience that so easily beset them, and replace them with confidence, strength, peace, happiness, wisdom and ultimately, *R.I.S.E.*

R.I.S.E. as in **R**ebuild **I**ntentionally and **S**trategically for **E**ffectiveness to a new level that is beneficial. Tam is confident that the tools that are being shared by those who have joined the movement, when used, will be an added tool that will assist in fixing those things that may have been broken as a result of the separation and/or divorce from one who you once believed it was till death do us apart.

Introduction

I have known Tamora "Tam" Burton, the founder of the Life After Divorce Movement for quite a few years now. We met at a mutual friends' think-tank meeting and have been connected since then. For years, I followed her social media page and realized that her purpose, passion, and mission was one that was needed, yet not many were openly speaking about it.

As I continued to follow Tam's work, it took a shift and began to grow where men were being included in the movement. I took interest in it because I was able to immediately recognize the change agents that she was providing in the community for those experiencing divorce. I slowly began to respond to her posts and shared that I would love to be a part of the movement that she so graciously uses: "lock arms." According to Tam, this term says, "If you are in agreement, let's serve each other in this season." When asked to be a part of this anthology, it was an honor, and I am excited to share my thoughts in regard to life during AND after divorce.

The ability to bounce back after a divorce lends to the resiliency of the person who has given their all in a failed relationship. One of the biggest challenges you will face is learning how to challenge yourself to improve on being a better you. The more you spend time wallowing in regret, the further away from upliftment and self-improvement you will be.

While children, young and older, don't want to see their parents separate or divorce, it is highly recommended that you have therapy set up with them. Children need to know that you are breaking apart from the other parent, and not divorcing them. It is vital for children to know the truth but only when they are mature enough to do so.

With this said, the individual must learn discretion is the better part of valor. These steps will lead to you coming full circle and regaining your joy and inner strength. The process includes redefining, reinvigorating, revitalizing, and recreating yourself by taking the necessary steps in becoming a much more improved version of yourself.

Another part is being ready to identify,

acknowledge, and approach a healthy relationship without all the hang-ups you were once plagued with. Your now discerning eye will be able to see a truly healthy relationship for what it is, a fertile ground for you to love and be loved...let's lock arms with Tam and consistently do the work and know that there is LIFE After DIVORCE!

Tool: God
The main tool required to have in your toolbox to fix anything that is broken.
#TamSaid

Reflecting on the journey of life after divorce, I can't help but take a glance at the moments leading up to that faithful walk down the aisle. I was just 22 years old, still figuring out life and what it had to offer. I had already fathered a child from a previous relationship at the early age of 19, and now a few years later, while still trying to grasp fatherhood, here I was taking on marriage. But this was not a strain for me because as a young child I always visualized myself being a proud father and husband, so it was not an encounter that I was trying to avoid.

As I transitioned into my first marriage, I had no idea what to expect but I courageously entered the lion's den, with hopes of success. We both entered the marriage relationship as damaged goods. She carried with her the brokenness of unresolved childhood traumas, insecurities, no high school education, and no zeal for God. The odds were stacked already because this young man had no clue how to deal with a young woman with those types of issues. To make it more complicated, I had my own unresolved childhood traumas that I was still trying to make sense of. With all the above factors in mind, you can imagine the issues of constant immature arguments we had in the beginning, which never led to any resolution and only resulted in confusion and verbal abuse on both sides.

Spiritual interventions were ineffective in our case because throughout the entire marriage relationship she exhibited no desire to connect with her spiritual nature, which stacked the odds even higher because what I did know for sure was that without God at the center, this was going to be a tough battle. Where could we possibly go from here but down? The insecurities progressively got worse, which oftentimes caught me off-guard because I had never encountered such scenarios in my young experience of relationships.

My first wife would often feed into her insecurities and would make statements to me like,

"You're too good to be true; I know you're out there doing something." This puzzled me as a young man because all I did was work, come home, and attend church on the weekends. She would check my receipts from the grocery store, to see which cities I traveled to, checking to see if I had traveled to cities and places that didn't add up in her mind.

The worst scenario I encountered with her insecurities happened on one occasion when she came to pick me up from work and she perceived that I was riding around in my company vehicle up to no good, with another female co-worker. She approached me and the female co-worker in a hostile manner before we could step out of the vehicle. She embarrassed me in front of my clients and co-workers, yelling and screaming and calling my co-worker out of her name, not to mention those clients were minor children that I mentored in a group home facility.

Unfortunately, those types of encounters continued. It became too unbearable to deal with. I reached my breaking point and asked for a divorce.

What I visualized as a young child of being a father and husband one day, turned out to be a disaster and not what I hoped it would be. To add insult to injury, I had no clue that moving into this next phase of the divorce process was going to be even worse.

I went through a rollercoaster of emotions at the onset of the divorce, feeling that I had failed my children and even worse feeling that I failed God. I suppressed my emotions by going to the casino, drinking, and gambling my life away. This was a terrible habit I developed during the marriage to manage stress.

I began to fall deeper and deeper into depression because it was not an easy decision for an active father such as myself to separate from my family and not be with my children every single day. When I thought things couldn't get worse, my first wife decided to take it up a notch and would verbally abuse me by calling me vulgar names, unjustly categorizing me as a "deadbeat dad" and she would often emotionally abuse my children by telling them I didn't want them anymore because I was divorcing her.

I was totally heartbroken and at the same time full of rage and anger. By the time the divorce was final, I was exhausted and had nothing left. I wasn't the loving, funny, and goofy father anymore to my children. I didn't desire to be in any more relationships and most importantly I struggled with my relationship with God. This led to me continuing to cope with my depression inappropriately, which later developed into a gambling addiction and resulted in my life hitting rock bottom.

There I was, at the bottom, and all I could do then was look up. It was at that time that God's voice became loud in my ears saying!

"My grace is sufficient for you, for my power is made perfect in your weakness," God said.

After living in my truck for two weeks, I finally swallowed my pride and called my mother. I told her everything. For the next year and a half, I isolated myself in a room at my mother's house and I began to listen to God. As God's children, we often forget that our bodies are the Temple of God in which the Spirit of God dwells within us. All we must do is hit the pause button and remove all the outside distractions, and the voice of God will turn up.

When I hit the pause button, God showed me a life that was purposeful for His name's sake. It was then that God put something on my heart, and I said to myself, "*I refuse to go back.*" I refuse to go back and revisit the brokenness of my past failures, resentment issues, and anger.

God left me with a plan in the form of the acronym "**I R**efuse **T**o **G**o **B**ack (IRTGB)." I followed this plan faithfully and it regenerated that positive energy and motivation I needed to move forward and live a productive and purposeful life.

(I) is for *Intentional*. Be intentional with every move you make. Set reachable and purposeful goals for yourself. Be intentional with removing negative energy and negative people from your life and replace them with positive energy and positive people in your life who have the same interest and goals you have set for yourself.

(R) is for *Renewing* your mind. Renew your mind daily through meditation and prayer and seek God's wisdom in every situation which will help you see life through the lens of an eternal purpose and not a temporary purpose of self-gratification.

(T) is for *Teaching* others about your testimony. Teaching others about your personal testimony is the most influential tool we possess to guide others on the right path to recovery. Your story will give hope and inspire others to keep fighting because through hearing your story they see that it is possible. Sharing your story continues your healing process and reveals how far you have come, and how far you must go.

(G) is for *Gratefulness*. A heart of gratefulness leads to humility. Be grateful for what you do have and do not worry about what you don't have. Be grateful that you are alive, be grateful for this moment and time that you have right now to get back on track if you so desire.

Our most valued asset in life is time. You can't worry or dwell on what happened yesterday because yesterday is a thing of the past and you can't change what happened. You can't worry about the future because we are not promised to see tomorrow. All we have is this time and moment right now to make an impact and effect positive change in our own life and others.

(B) is for *Believing* in yourself. Believe that you are more than capable because there is a power that is working inside of you, that is able to do exceedingly and abundantly above all that we can ask or even imagine. God gave you the ability, which means success is guaranteed.

After God blessed me with this plan ("I Refuse To Go Back"), He then gifted me with a second chance, by sending some accessories to go along with it. He provided for me a beautiful wife, with a heart of gold, and a true zeal for God. If God's will be done, my wife and I will be celebrating this year our 10-year marriage anniversary and the butterflies are still very much present. We have a total of seven beautiful children combined and life has come full circle for me because one of the sweetest parts of the story is that I was able to experience having all my children live with me in harmony under one roof, something I thought would never be possible.

With that being said, the happy ending to the story has little to do with me. It has everything to do with the goodness of God. Every good and perfect gift comes from God and the purpose of those gifts is to serve the Kingdom.

Tool: Level
All things that occur during the divorce must have harmony, otherwise there will be an imbalance in how you navigate it.
#TamSaid

In my opinion, to a certain degree, life is what you make it. Life after divorce is really no different. Like the saying goes, *"you get out what you put in,"* I personally went through different stages of emotions along my journey before ultimately settling into a place of peace.

Denial, confusion, finger pointing, reflection, depression, were some of the many stages I found myself facing. I would have my good days, then other days I wouldn't even want to get out of bed. I was always taught tough times don't last long, but tough people do. Life might've knocked me down, but I was determined to get back on my feet.

Although I was a product of divorce, it didn't make the process of recovery any easier. If anything, for me, it made it more challenging. I had once vowed to never put my children through the pain and dysfunction I experienced when my parents divorced. Sometimes what we think we want isn't exactly what we need. Sometimes we realize the life we want isn't meant to be with the person we chose. Or sometimes it may be just as simple as two people growing apart and the work that's required to make it work wasn't being put forth. Regardless of the circumstances, D - Day was upon me, along with the aftermath.

I knew it wasn't going to be easy. Looking back, I was nowhere near properly prepared for what was to come. I went from married with three kids to a single father overnight. Thank God I had a solid foundation and support system. My grandma would always say it takes a village to raise a child. The assistance my mother and grandmother provided for me with my children during this transition was huge. Helping check the kids into new schools, home cooked meals, overall, just providing a sense of comfort and normalcy for me and my babies during this tough time.

Although family was there for us, I could tell my children were struggling with the changes in their lives. I decided to seek professional counseling for us, which proved to be a great decision. I think my teenage daughter benefited the most from her one-on-one sessions. In all honesty, it was kind of disheartening to me, for my child to be more willing to express her feelings to a complete stranger than her own father.

Once I was able to get over that and be open minded to the therapist's suggestions, things started improving. Slowly, but surely. By no means was this the end all be all. There would be many more obstacles to overcome. Plenty of tear-filled nights with my children asking why, plenty of rebellious moments, a few moments of testing my gangsta. I learned to lead with love and exercise patience.

Just like each one of my kid's personalities are different, this divorce seemed to affect and take a toll on them differently. It was and is my job to make sure they have the right environment and opportunities that are conducive to them healing as individuals before we can truly heal as a family. As stated before, my teenage daughter seemed to benefit most from counseling. My oldest son found refuge in church and his two grandmothers.

This life after divorce thing is a marathon, not a sprint, especially when children are a part of the equation. I continue to encourage my children to openly express their feelings. Whether it's to a parent, family member, counselor, pastor, journaling, etc. Just don't bottle up those emotions. It's ok to cry, it's ok to be sad, just know that life ain't perfect and regardless of the cards you were dealt, life goes on. Love yourself first, then love those who love you!

I did a whole lot of praying and a whole lot of debating with myself asking was it worth it. The answer is, *absolutely*! In no way, shape, or form, has my life after divorce been easy, but it's most definitely been beautiful.

It ain't how you start, it's how you finish! Everything I asked God for, He sent me in my new wife, and some! If you thought divorce was difficult, try being a blended family. But I was built for this. God places his toughest battles on His strongest soldiers.

I am now happily the husband/father of a blended family of five children. Life has its challenges; life after divorce is no different. Your life is what *you* make it! The choice is yours! You can choose to be bitter, or you can choose to be better!

Tool: Hammer

*"To the man who only has a hammer, everything he
encounters begins to look like a nail."*
~ Abraham Maslow paraphrasing an earlier quote from
Abraham Kaplan

Divorce, much like marriage, tends to be a life-altering
event, but divorce is not the end of the world. The
challenging experiences of divorce and recreation can
be a complicated, painful, and a crazy time. Even so,
there is life *after* divorce.

Divorce will take you outside your comfort
zone, but your journey is not over. Instead, you've
reached a place where it's time for you to process your
grief and reconnect with yourself and who you want

to be.

I have been married and divorced three times, however, to only two women. How does that happen, you ask? It happens when you're a glutton for punishment and marry the same person twice!

I am a humble and steady believer that there is life after divorce, so rather than becoming incredibly angry and disillusioned after each divorce, I took time by myself to reflect on learning about who I was underneath all of the roles I played. While divorce may be harder on men, acquiring the tools needed during the difficult transition of going through the emotional turmoil of a divorce and living with the pain lingering in the aftermath allows you to become more attuned to the opportunities and possibilities available.

Divorce #1: Even the darkest nights come to an end, and the Sun will rise

After moving out of state and halfway across the country, I met and married my first wife in the summer of 2000. Our relationship was tumultuous from the start and never seemed to even out. Even so, I held on to the notion that a baby could save the marriage. We welcomed our daughter into the world just under two years later.

Still, my wife and I continued to have the same fights repeatedly. It was mainly because without realizing it I was extremely self-centered and egotistical with several yet-to-be-diagnosis and consequently untreated mental health issues at the time. While some believe it is best to stay together for the kids, the relationship was severely strained after almost six years of marriage.

I asked for a divorce because I believed our daughter would be better off with parents who were happier apart than unhappy together. Moreover, I wanted her to grow up with a healthy view of love in practice. The divorce process itself was relatively painless because my wife at the time was an attorney – I asked for what belonged to me before we got married and told her that she could keep the rest, including the house, car, and full custody of our daughter – and she filed the divorce papers.

While the duration from filing a petition to getting a final court judgment in most divorces averages about a year, the timeframe is significantly decreased in uncontested divorces, like ours, taking only about three months. Our divorce was finalized in the month following her filing the divorce papers.

Divorce #2: Out with the old, in with the new
I met my second wife in the spring of 2006. However, we didn't start dating until the fall of 2007 and were married in the fall of 2008. Like my first marriage, it was tumultuous from the start and never seemed to even out due to several factors, including, but not limited to, her not working throughout the majority of our one-and-a-half-year marriage, leaving me financially

responsible for her two children from a prior relationship and us. Not only were we embroiled in a search for affordable, long-term stable housing, but this coincided with when I struggled to remain in any one position for very long because I was busy chasing the almighty dollar to provide for my family.

These complexities led to us being homeless – having to couch surf just to have a roof over our heads. This ultimately placed us in a position where we felt compelled to give her two young daughters, both under the age of two at the time, up for adoption. As all parents do, we felt that our children deserved a better life than we were going to be able to provide them.

After placing the children up for adoption, my satisfaction with the marriage started to wane. We divorced in the summer of 2010. Ultimately, my income was insufficient to save our family or marriage.

Oddly enough, the first ex-wife helped me divorce the second wife. Again, I only asked for what belonged to me before we got married and told her that she could keep the rest, which seeing as we had nothing, sadly, she got nothing. Also, like my previous divorce, my second divorce was finalized the month following the filing of the divorce papers.

Divorce #3: Fool me once, shame on you; fool me twice, shame on me

Following my divorce from my second wife, I elected to move out-of-state, again; however, an old employer offered me a position to run one of his businesses, so I returned to where I came from. In addition to returning to the state, my first ex-wife and I rekindled our relationship and remarried, whereby my first wife became my third wife.

Out with the old and in with the older, right? After getting divorced again from the same woman, I concluded I was a glutton for punishment. Let me stop here because I'm getting ahead of myself. Let's return to the actual cause of the divorce and the divorce process itself.

During this marriage, since the kids had aged some – she had a second child, a son, with another man during the time we were divorced. I had opted to stay together, even during the most turbulent of times of our troubled marriage, for the sake of the kids. I thought that the kids deserved a two-parent home environment, despite the continuous state of conflict, instability, argumentation, hatred, and uncertainty.

In addition to rekindling our marriage, I relapsed in my addiction after ten years of sobriety. I remained a functioning, active addict for the remainder of our marriage. While I had learned to communicate better, the coupling of my substance abuse and a particularly traumatic life experience that went unspoken for fifteen years were among the leading contributors to our second (and final!) divorce from one another after being remarried for almost eleven additional years.

Critical Tools: Fully equipped with the tools to fulfill our purpose

"Always remember that you are braver than you believe, stronger than you seem, smarter than you think, and loved more than you know." ~ Christopher Robin to Pooh, *Winnie the Pooh*

What can you do to help yourself move on? Reflecting on the lessons of a divorce can help turn your emotions, like anger and shame, into a commitment to grow. Take a good look at yourself and own your part in the relationship's failure.

The time it takes to recover from a divorce emotionally depends on a variety of factors. This includes whether you saw the split coming, whether it was your choice, whether you were left for another person, whether you have kids, whether you are self-supporting, whether you're getting adequate help, and whether you have the right resources and information around you, but employing specific tools may help.

In the process of finding myself and becoming comfortable in my skin, I learned many valuable and critical tools needed to survive and thrive after divorce. Don't ignore how you feel; remember that change is always tricky, and you will find happiness again if you can learn to let go and don't let your past write your future, and don't keep providing fuel for your negative emotions:

Don't ignore how you feel

Ignoring your true feelings can be devastating to your well-being — making it easier for intense negative emotions like resentment or anger to fester and grow, causing anxiety and depression to blossom. Allowing yourself to feel and give yourself time and permission to grieve at the end of the relationship is healthy. Let yourself be where you are, and don't rush through the grieving process or pretend to be further along than you are.

Remember that change is always tricky

Change can sometimes feel overwhelming. It's a great idea to tackle things methodically, write a to-do list and take it one task at a time instead of feeling overwhelmed by your uncertain future. It will feel less scary and far more manageable.

Remember that you will find happiness again

Divorce can provide the ideal opportunity for growth and self-discovery. Now is the perfect time to rediscover what makes you happy and plan for the future, which will help propel you through the healing process.

Don't keep on providing fuel for your negative emotions

It would help if you found a healthy way to cope with your feelings. Dwelling on what went wrong or the circumstances that led to your divorce will only keep you trapped in a negative head space that won't facilitate your healing, so work on acceptance.

Life will never give you more than you can handle. By putting these tools in place, you will be on your way to a full recovery. Once we start recognizing the truth of our story, we can be decisive when choosing our destination, so the universe can provide us with the tools we need to reach it.

Keep these tools with you and get out there and create a masterpiece. Never let the future disturb you. We cannot change the past, but we can start a new chapter with a happy ending.

Divorce is not the end of the world. In your life after divorce, you might not know how you want to rebuild your life or what you want to fill it with. Still, you have the opportunity and the tools to transcend from a disempowered mindset of existence to an empowered reality of purpose-driven living. You have the tools, now get out there and dare to discover the art of reinvention and the marvelous things awaiting you!

Tool: Utility knife
Sometimes you have to be brave enough to cut things
off and out that are no longer needed.
#TamSaid

During the divorce, the mother of my child accused me of being physically abusive to her and she said in court papers that she suspected me of molesting our child. I've never expressed this in writing nor spoken it out loud, until now. There! I've said it finally.

Life after divorce after *that* accusation to close friends and family and the spreading of that story left me feeling some kind of way. I was falsely accused. I felt humiliated, condemned, and distanced from those who knew me, and our situation knew it was false. Yet, they withdrew not wanting to get involved in our legal mess. In fact, I lost a lot of emotional support. Life after my divorce was solitary and lonely.

I know that you're probably expecting me to relay a story of triumph and success of overcoming insurmountable odds in climbing to the top of the mountain and raising my hands skyward shouting HALLELUJAH, Thank you, JESUS! No. That hasn't been the case for me. Yes, I've built a business. Yes, I am doing what I love. Yes, it has allowed me opportunities to work in the child development field. I work in the industry called individual and family counselling, where every day I get to change people's lives, yet, mine had been in most need of change.

When I reflect on the years that have gone by post-divorce, I think of years of loss, shame, and deep regret. Sadness, the deepest depression, anxiety, and worry have worn me like a second skin. I have born this weight and worn it well. No one knows how much pain I have been in. Because of Jesus, I have born pain, my cross, and compassion. This dichotomy may seem perplexing to some but for those who understand forgiveness, they understand how you can feel compassion for the harm done to you by one's previous spouse, while at the same time working through the harm they have dealt us.

At times, as I worked through the deep hurt, recovering myself, getting up in the mornings was very hard. At least that's how it's been up to November of last year. In November, after attending the Life After

Divorce conference, everything began to shift and turn around. I came not bearing unforgiveness nor resentment. I came with that luggage packed. Everything washed, bleached, fabric softened, and neatly folded. I came to leave those bags! Praise GOD, I DID!!!

Going into that conference, I had recently come out of a 40-day fast that began the year prior ending in January of the conference year. Yes, I did deep cleaning during that fast. Released an addictive behavior that I turned to release the sadness whenever it was triggered. I began nurturing boundaries, setting limits, and finding healthy ways to manage stress.

During that conference, I experienced tremendous healing. I literally left a self behind and returned home a changed person! I began a new life of restoration, recovery, and recuperation. Life after divorce prior to that had been regret and loss. I experienced a plethora of negative feelings and emotions since my divorce concluded in October of 2006.

I married a woman that I shouldn't have. She married a man that she shouldn't have. I packed all those feelings and thoughts over the year and was READY for the conference.

Both of us came from people who should never have dated and made children. We married because it seemed like the right thing to do, but neither one of us was whole, mature, or ready. We were just fragments of other people's broken, miserable selves. Other people's regrets and losses poured into us and drew us together. It was wholly a co-dependent relationship. I processed and packed up that too!

My mom and my dad never married. During the time my spouse was in my life, my mother did everything she could to alienate my spouse. It was ridiculous how cold and disrespectful she was to my son's mother. I wanted their relationship to work so bad that I literally turned a blind eye to the cold treatment.

I was born when my mother was 16 years of age. My father was 17 years of age. My spouse's mom and dad married when people should marry, and they had the life that married people have. They divorced. Neither one of us came from whole people or healthy people who knew who they were, where they were going, and how to get there. Neither one of us came from people who really trusted God, believed in God, or served God. I'm not here to focus on her, her mother, nor her father, because that's her story, yet her history and mine affected our walk and our talk. This too, I put in the washer, let it run through all cycles, then dried, folded. Some items I had to steam iron and press out before it lay rested, neat, and foldable. Eventually, all that got packed. This was several suitcases worth of baggage. I left that behind, too.

I reflect on when I experienced the deepest pain in the deepest pit of sorrow with regard to regret. It was when I received court documents accusing me of having sexually molested my child and here's what the document said: *My son saw white stuff coming out of my penis. He said my penis looked like a banana.* That's what the court document said, and it went on to say how she discovered this sexually immoral act. They were sitting at breakfast and my son refused to eat a banana. Now when we were married my son never liked eating anything soft or mushy. He would never eat bananas. The only time my son has ever seen my penis was when he opened the bathroom door and walked in on me while I was in the bathroom urinating. Yes I was accused, and this has been the deepest, darkest shadow lurking in my life.

If you have never been accused of molestation, then you have no idea of the emotional pain it comes with. Being accused in court and having that told to friends and family is nearly as bad as being true! In the minds of those who hear it, they NEVER look at you the same. It's a struggle when you look into the eyes of your family and friends as they try to shake free of it; but, when it comes from the other parent, the question arises: *Why would they say that*? I saw them trying to reconcile these images of me. I saw how it led them to just walk away. That's what happened to me.

During the months prior to the conference, I had to wash board these rags. Bent over the tub. Scrub. Scrub. Stains so hard to come out. Layers deep. Scrub. Scrub. I had to replace the water several times. Get it scalding hot. I sweat. Cried. Poured out my soul to

GOD asking WHY? What did I do to earn this!? Scrub. Scrub. Over time, the stains lessened to white. The grime fell away. The stank came out. The water eventually stopped darkening. I was finally able to wring rinse this load by hand. I could fit this in a dryer.

Everything here was hung dry old style. Outside for all to see. The sun poured down, warmed, and dried these lines of clipped laundry. With basked under arm, item by item, was removed from the clothesline. I took it inside and neatly folded every issue lovingly, kindly, and gently. Every piece packed away in trunks. Several trunks worth of things. I left those things back there in Sun City.

At that conference, I backed up that truck and unloaded every item in that conference room and at the breakfast table. During the dinner. Laid some in my room. Down the hallway. A few found their way into the elevator. I left a few in baggage claim. None it belonged to me anymore, so, I didn't care. I got back in the truck and drove away. I've NEVER looked back!

Life after divorce had been an experience of living under that accusation and never being able to dispel it. In many ways, I have been vindicated by time; however, that single accusation tore my life to pieces. I've spent over 15 years putting it back together. In this time, I've had to deal with it being brought up in court documents, her testimony, and with my son present to hear it. It's the gun she slings and the bullet she fires when desperate that things aren't going her way. Shame. Shame me in acquiescence or persuade a judge to rule in her favor.

Once a year in or around October, I get a summons to appear. Over the years, I've experienced this shame. She's homeless, living in a van, along with my son and unable to find employment because of her illness. I've been investigated for this sexual immoral act by the local police and by the Attorney General's office and I've been vindicated. Every time we go to court, she loses. After a while, I got summoned again. It's a new judge. She gets a new audience. She gets a chance to call me a convicted pedophile in her minutes of presenting her case. Even though it isn't true, that label still cuts through me. The accusation itself is damaging. New ears have to search it out. Thank GOD for internet and at hands data bases. I've seen judges fingers flurry over keys. Look up and give that, LETS MOVE ON look, but say: Is there anything else?

While it does cut, it does not cut deep just leaves a crease on the skin that eventually goes away. I had to hire a team of professional cleaners. This was a crime, a murder scene. I felt eviscerated. There was blood and gore everywhere soaked into everything. The people you call when you can't do it yourself. The professionals. The cleaning and washing were so thorough it seemed no crime was committed. They used a flatbed to lay all this on. I drove the flatbed and backed it up and unloaded it onto the golf course near the hotel I stayed in. Never looked back!

My ex has a master's degree from University of

California at Berkeley, in public health, This is the person who made this accusation against the father of her child during our divorce proceedings. Why? Answer: It happens all the time in family court. It is the single most damaging accusation levelled against fathers. It's a frequently used allegation in family court proceedings by mothers. The second most damaging is an accusation of spousal abuse. Domestic violence. Yes. She went there as well. As a result, she won temporary custody. It was temporary and became permanent because I was too broken to fight.

The truth is *she* is mentally ill. She's been diagnosed several times and each time she always finds someone to reverse the diagnosis. Mental illness is genetic.

You might be thinking: He hates this woman. That is not the case. She is the mother of my son and for that I will always love her. Remember, that dichotomy I mentioned earlier? I carry the deepest forgiveness for her. I haven't been idle over the years. I turned my scars into badges. I am a certified personal development coach, a domestic violence treatment counselor, and an anger management & parenting coach. I've worked through my issues and triumphed over them.

Through the years, I've helped and coached many people through the same tragedies. I am in the individual and family counseling industry, clean background, fingerprinted and certified by the Department of Justice. My business is an approved provider within the family court system. I guess in some small way time has vindicated me, but that accusation has been a cloud over my head in my mind.

This is my final act. The laundry is cleaned, packed, and discarded. Now, I am slamming the door shut! I'm tired of walking under its shadow, fearful of her popping up to disrupt my life. I refuse to give her that power. I finally disperse it, dissipate, and cancel it in Jesus' name! While it has not impeded my career, the hurt over it has hobbled me from trusting, opening up, and letting people into my life.

I miss my son. That's the second biggest regret. He and I have spent zero time together. I've lacked the energy of will to produce the intensity to tread over and overcome the shadow. And as a result of my lack of force, my lack of fight, I have allowed it to become a real thing. Maybe in his mind, maybe in the minds of some, but publicly in my industry it doesn't exist.

What I wanted to make clear here is that I am not a victim and I want to make it clear to my son if he should ever read this: *You are not a victim*. I also want to apologize to him for not being there, for not standing up for him, not fighting for him, not resisting, not fighting back, for not storming the castle walls to bring him into my life. That's regret number three.

There was a weakness in me to fight against, pursue, and overcome every obstacle that his mom has laid in front of me to get him into my life. I've had many opportunities to build, to overcome, to fight back, and resist; however, I've always been reluctant to do so and I know exactly where that comes from. It comes from a broken place in me where I adopted the attitudes, behaviors, and mannerisms of my father who never fought for me. It's a legacy that was passed down to me annoyingly. Nevertheless, I adopted it unknowingly.

I am not blaming my father. I'm just simply talking about why the behavior has been in me. It's been a place of emptiness and weakness - a vacuous void. A void that I could have turned over to God many times over. I could've trusted in God to fill it and then been healed of it, but I've been reluctant even stubbornly to guard it.

Life after divorce. I've rarely dated. I have one or two close friends. But I've largely hidden myself beneath business and behind my business. Working long hours. Only coming out of my work environment for breakfast lunch or dinner. I've been reluctant to invite people into my life to share my personality and enjoy others. Life after divorce for me up until recently has sucked.

After last year's Life *After* Divorce conference, I've purchased all new emotional and spiritual real-estate. I can smell the fresh new scent on everything. The space is cleared now. Ready to be furnished! It's a palatial mansion, full of transparency, honesty, openness, and plenty of room for someone else. Things are looking up.

How many years has it been since my divorce? It concluded in 2006 and now it's 2023. I am very much looking forward to sharing my testimony at the next conference. There are many things on my dream board that will manifest between now and then.

I am finally coming out of my cave of shadow and stepping into the light of the Son of Righteousness. I am finally bathed in salvation and freedom. I am looking forward to the new life unfolding because it's been long years laboring in the dark, repairing, healing, fixing, and being restored. Now, I am finally emerging!

Tool: Flashlight
Reflecting on self illuminates light into an area of darkness and begins to brighten it.
#TamSaid

I was a very troubled young man. I was taking my life down a spiral of no return. Me and the mother of my children were not getting along. The relationship was very toxic and was very unhealthy for the both of us.

We had a fight, and it wasn't pretty. I was cheating on her with other women that I had met along the way. I was arrogant and at this time in my life I felt I was God's gift to women.

I came home from work, and it was late. I

worked the 2 pm to 10 pm shift. When I got home, it was around 11:30 pm. I opened the door and saw my kid's mother sitting on the couch. I went to give her a kiss on the forehead, and she pushed my face back. I knew from there I was in trouble. There were a hundred thoughts going on in my head. I wondered what I had been caught doing this time.

I went into our bedroom, got undressed, took a shower, and came back to the living room. I could see the disgust all over her face. She got up and said she was going to bed. I stayed in the living room and was channel surfing on the television so I could find something to watch. No later than 10 minutes "CRACK!" I was hit upside my head with a hard object. I immediately felt the lump on my head rising.

"WHAT'S YOUR FUCKING PROBLEM!"

She said, "You're my problem!"

The fight was on. The neighbors called the cops, and they arrived within three minutes. We lived in a middle-class neighborhood, so they always came quick. They asked what was going on and they saw the big ass knot on my head. I didn't want to say anything to incriminate myself, so I chose to be silent.

They attempted to put my kid's mother in handcuffs, then I spoke up. I told the cops that I hit her, and she retaliated against me. Protecting her from going to jail, I took the hit for the sake of the kids. Even though I was wrong for getting caught once again for my infidelities, I had to take the domestic violence charge.

I spent 11 days in jail. I ended up pleading to a deal of 45 days' work release, with 11 days credit, with summary probation. I didn't want to go back home so I went to live with my mom until things cooled off at home.

I went to the barbershop by my mom's house for a new fade haircut. Usually, the owner of the barber shop would cut my hair, but this time he let his new employee cut my hair. The new stylist was a woman, and her name was Venus. I never let a woman cut my hair so this would be the first. I sat in the chair, she got me ready, and I told her what kind of hair cut I wanted, and she began to cut.

She did a wonderful job; she did a way better cut than the owner did. So, every time I would get my hair cut, I went to her. Venus was a very gorgeous woman. I could see why her mother named her Venus because she was out of this world. I noticed me and Venus started having chemistry. Her conversations were very deep like I never heard from a woman before.

We started conversing outside the barbershop and the owner low key didn't like it, but what was he going to do, he was a married man and his wife was his business partner. Things started getting heated between me and Venus in a passionate way. We began dating and before you know it, we were an item. Me and my kids' mother were having problems, some of it was her fault but the majority of it was mines. I wasn't going back home so I left it at that. I made sure my kids were taken care of and did my duties as a father.

Venus had her dream of opening her own shop. She was very smart and very ambitious. A few weeks into dating she asked me did I want to go to church with her, and I agreed to go. I ended up going to church with her every Tuesday, Thursday, and Sunday. I was praying and I learned how to speak in tongues. I was now a member of this church.

I was in love with Venus. We had so much in common it was crazy. Three months into the relationship, I asked Venus to marry me, and she said yes. We didn't have money for a wedding at that time, so we ended up going to city hall and getting married. The ring I got her was two-carats. It wasn't much but she was very happy and grateful. I told my mom I was married, and my mom was happy. She liked Venus a great deal. I liked Venus' parents. Her dad was quiet, but her mom was the most amazing woman I ever met. She would hold my hand and she would read my past and my future. This woman knew things about me I never told anyone. She was so spot on I can't lie I began to cry because she knew all the pain that I was feeling inside. She became my mentor, and she would tell me about the evil things going on at the church me and her daughter were attending. She said she would warn Venus, but Venus wouldn't listen. She would point things out to me and would show me things through my inner vision I had never seen before.

I started to see the warning signs each time I

attended this church. It was like the spell I was under was wearing off and I started seeing things that Venus' mom would tell me to look for. I no longer wanted to be a part of this church. They were preaching more about money than they were God, and I didn't like that at all.

I told my wife, and she didn't want to hear it. By this time Venus was pregnant and we were expecting our first child. I was very excited, and I was looking forward to sharing a life and a child with Venus. When I quit the church, me and Venus' relationship had took a wrong turn. She was upset that she had to go to church alone, pregnant, and her husband wasn't there. Her mom would tell her if your husband doesn't want to go then you shouldn't want to go. But she had her mind made up that she was going to be loyal to her congregation and she wasn't about to give her loyalty up for me and no one else.

At one time, my wife was out there in the world and this particular church helped her change her life around. For a short period of time, it did wonders for me as well. But for me I wasn't about to break the bank for these people. I had kids to support and a wife that was pregnant with my child.

A few months went by and me and Venus began to talk less and less. It was making me upset that she was more loyal to her church than me. Had I known this in the beginning I would never have taken the relationship with Venus this far.

My kids' mother would talk to me because she did know me better than any other woman I have dealt with in my life. She really wanted me to come back home and in a way I did want to go back home. But I didn't want to be in no more toxic nonsense that me and her always had.

I could tell these church goers were all in Venus' ear. She became extra distant. I got a call at work one day and it was Venus telling me she had lost the baby. I was devastated because in reality I loved her, and I wanted my first marriage to last.

Her church was so much in her ear the marriage just fell apart. And I took it upon myself to get the marriage annulled. That was that, we were done. She went her way, and I went mines. We ended up seeing each other a few years later. She had a new husband, two kids, and she had finally opened her own shop. I was happy for her.

I ended up having another child with my kids' mother and we ended up getting married when I came home from jail. But that within itself is another story.

False love can come in different shapes, sizes, and colors. I always knew I was a very difficult man, and I was always stubborn and did things my way. I refused to be miserable and seeing how mean those people were in that church and the way they manipulated people and the way they talked bad about people, it was no different than what you hear on the streets. But these are supposed to be God fearing Christian folk. Yet behind the mask and the smile was nothing but greed, betrayal, and scandal.

I went to Venus shop a few times to get my hair cut but I knew it wasn't the right thing for me to keep doing so I stopped going. Cause all we would talk about was the mistakes we made in our marriage. It wasn't like we were going to get back together and work things out. She had a whole family and so did I. After that I never heard or talked to Venus again.

Me and my current wife were married for 12 years. The relationship spanned off and on for 20 years. Unfortunately, she passed away due to clogged arteries to the heart. I strongly advise people to take better care of yourself because you never know. My wife passed away at 34 years of age and on the outside she looked beautiful and healthy. Never take life for granted because you never know when the grim reaper is going to be knocking at your door.

Tool: _Tape measurer_
Track your happiness and peace through doing
the things that you love
#TamSaid

Author's Note
(from the Introduction in _Finding The Elixir_):

"When we're at our lowest points in life, thinking negatively, and seemingly without hope, new opportunities often present themselves right on time. Sometimes we just need the courage to step out of our comfort zone, have faith in humanity and explore. A dash of luck doesn't hurt either."

So how does a person meet amazing people, travel to incredible places, and experience some of the greatest moments of their life after a painful divorce forced a complete shift in circumstances and priorities? The answers are in the chapters of my book, *Finding The Elixir*. My hope is that you find these stories entertaining, meaningful and uplifting. They are all true.

We all know life is about growth. After divorce, I allowed myself to "spread my wings" through travel and the experiences helped me learn and grow in significant ways. I traveled while happily married, but not enough for my taste. And after hearing from my wife that she was not happily married enough for her taste, I needed an escape. Not an escape toward denial, but an escape toward a place where I could look back on my 18-year relationship and my life and ask honestly, "What the hell happened?"

Use this book as a travel guide—one written for the journey of your heart and mind. May it bring you to much more than iconic landmarks along the way; may it also help you pursue and find the happiness we all truly deserve.

Excerpt from my book:

Travel and Gratitude
Being open and grateful for the opportunity to travel when it presented itself, I started taking chances my previous self would've thought foolish. And doing so provided some amazing experiences which served as a catalyst to my

future chapters. Being divorced allowed me to rediscover some passions I had for baseball and travel, which helped me move forward. Being single again and no longer having to explain why I wanted to do this or that was definitely an adjustment for me. Getting used to my new single status was extremely liberating because it offered a glimpse ahead at an independence I would come to embrace but hadn't felt for many years.

Opportunities and friendships can be fleeting in life. As a result, one of my post-divorce mantras became: do things when you can, while you can. Why wait until retirement to chase some dreams and travel adventures? We should all take some chances and be grateful we did. Alternatively, we can safely remain in our comfort zones and be fine. But I began feeling myself changing and taking on more of a growth mindset, which is essentially believing that each of us is in control of improving our abilities and situations.

My journey toward transitioning into learning more about who I was as a newly single guy and where I could go in life—both literally and figuratively—was beginning to take off. I've met some great people and have seen some amazing cities, landscapes, and sunsets throughout my travels—before and after my divorce. Showing and expressing gratitude—verbally and through actions—are vitally important, and I try to make sure the people I'm around know they are appreciated. I've always believed the more gratitude you show, the more you'll appreciate the good things in life rather than dwelling on the not-so-good aspects.

Showing and expressing gratitude to people isn't difficult, and it's a very powerful way of connecting as humans. By being grateful—whether through words or actions—you're showing someone they matter to you and you're not taking their kindness for granted. The bottom line is, we all deserve the best in life. I realized that feeling and expressing as much gratitude as possible and then paying it forward when you are able to is a winning combination. Your life and the lives around you will be positively impacted, which is ultimately good for everyone.

My divorce demoralized me and left me feeling broken in many ways. It obviously left me feeling despair on several levels, too. However, I came to realize how fortunate I was to have been given the opportunity of traveling with friends, family, and alone. Having hopes and dreams is vital, especially during important transition periods in our lives and everyone deserves to have them in life. Hope keeps us motivated and focused on better things in our future chapters.

I was constantly experiencing new things with people I was fortunate to meet after my divorce. I was extremely fortunate to find hope and begin dreaming again during a difficult transition period, and it made all the difference in my life going forward. The process of moving on was not easy and I had a lot of help from friends and family. They reminded me that challenges should make, but not break us. (Again, easier said than done.)

Learning from the challenges we face makes us stronger people, even if it may not feel that way at times. Gratitude and hope are extremely important, and I began fully appreciating the uplifting power of both as my growth process—and life—continued to unfold. Traveling was my way of facing the past, healing in the present, and looking forward to the future. Hopefully, it can help others do the same.

Tool: Saw
Cut it off and let it go when it's time.
Going back to unhealed places is unhealthy.
#TamSaid

Technically, we were together for 23 years. Married for 21 of those years but to be honest the decline in the marriage was building up for 15 years or more. I know you're thinking _why did you stay for so long_? The short answer is I didn't want a failed marriage on my resume.

I'm guilty of trying to uphold the image of a happily married man. Truth be told, I was miserable. The strain of trying to find a connection and being met with rejection every attempt took its toll on my mental health. I didn't recognize it at the time, but I was slowly falling into depression.

Over the years, everything I was passionate about started to sit on the shelf. It became hard to do the things I loved. We drifted further and further apart. My garage became a man cave, but ultimately more like a studio apartment where I spent most of my time. I was tired of all the name calling and having to take all the blame for everything wrong in our relationship.

Her words cut sharper than a 1095 carbon steel katana. She repeatedly told me over the years that I wasn't worthy of love, and I didn't deserve to be with anyone. She would find ways to hurt me with her words and to invoke rage inside me knowing I'm a peaceful person. Then, she'd point the finger at me and play victim.

She called me a rage monster because I would throw things out of frustration of not being heard. Constantly being called a liar when I'm telling the truth - that was infuriating. I fell deeper into depression and became more distant to the point I shut down. I'm a very attentive husband and father, but eventually I lived in my mind and didn't care about anything anymore. It all came to a head, and she filed for divorce.

Despite being miserable in the marriage it hit me even harder once she officially filed. The energy in the house over the next month while she got her affairs in order was hellish. I drank heavily. In my mind it was DEFCON one. Nuclear war was going off in my head and I wanted it all to end. I was completely out of my character and feeding into all the projections being hurled at me by the ex. It was all a blur. I couldn't see two inches in front of me. I was a ball of emotions and had lost all hope.

I didn't know if I would make it through the first night after she and our daughter moved out. The house was empty and so was my soul. If not for my friends I cannot say with confidence I would still be here. I'm usually the one people come to when they are having a hard time in life. Needless to say, I struggled with being vulnerable, but devastation of this magnitude I couldn't hide.

It was a shock to everyone that my ex and I were getting divorced. We hid it well. It was also a shock to see me in my darkest hour, but my brothers didn't hesitate to jump into action and be the shoulder I needed. I leaned on each and every one of them. I saw the true color in people. I saw how much my real ones cared for me. They cried with me, then made me laugh. They gave me pep talks, as well as sat in silence when I needed it. Just being there was enough.

My ex and I had not talked for months, but something special was coming up. One of my best friends was finally getting married. My ex had also known my boys for our entire relationship. They spent many days over our house. She was *sis* to them, and they were *bro* to her.

Out of all my friends, she did not get along with

any of their wives except this friends' soon to be wife. To squeeze lemon juice on our open wounds, they were getting married the same week as our anniversary. The divorce paperwork was already signed, sealed, and delivered, but technically we were still married for the next few months.

She reached out to see if I was going to the wedding. I had told my bro I didn't know if I could do it. My emotions were too unstable. He understood, but definitely wanted me there. It was the same for her and her friend, but we were both in the stage of grief. Reeling from the loss of 23 years of life. We both decided to go, separately.

I asked if I could give her a hug when we saw each other to show we were mature about this, and she declined. I had been holding on to the hope that after a few years apart and slowly working on things that we would get back together. I ask again *why*, when I knew she couldn't love me how I needed to be loved. It was the familiarity, the comfort zone, the trauma bond. I would rather go back to a known life of unhappiness, then to explore the unknown realms and find the person who was truly made for me.

I saw her briefly at the ceremony. The plan was to only attend the ceremony, then head back home. Quick pleasant greetings exchanged, then I surrounded myself with my friends and did my best to not focus on my situation and to be there for my guy.

I drove down with another close friend who had to work that night, so it worked out perfect. The only thing is when the brotherhood gets together it is hard for us to leave. My buddy called out of work, so party night was on.

Hours later, drinking and dancing, I got a text from my ex asking if I was still at the wedding. I said yes and asked why. She ended up getting a room at the hotel. The weight of the event and the timing of it all was emotionally too much for her to drive two hours back home. I asked if I could come see her and she agreed.

I didn't know what to expect. Leading into this we had not communicated well. It was still toxic. For the first time in a long time, we had a decent conversation. Emotions were high and we hooked up. It led to a week straight of her coming back over to my house and having sex.

She wanted to keep it secret, mainly because she had been bashing me to the world, but I didn't mind. As far as I was concerned we were finally starting to fix things. It was going to be the marriage I always envisioned.

When our friends got back from their honeymoon, my friends' wife told my ex the boys were saying we hooked up at the wedding. To be honest, of course I told my friends. I was excited. The way I disappeared that night without saying anything to anyone, they were looking for me. The other girls knew my ex had got a room and they all put two and two together. Either way, my ex was upset and lied to her friend that it didn't happen. She stopped talking with me for two weeks. I respected her boundaries and left her alone all the while working on my healing.

A few weeks before my birthday, she reached back out and we started to hang out again, in secret. Going to the beach, having lunch, movie dates, and sex, a whole relationship, again. By this point, I had been in therapy for almost nine months. I was different. I was no longer the person I had to be to survive in our marriage. I was finding myself, again.

After almost a month of secretly being together, I realized that she was the same person. The same person that mentally broke me down and I could not go back to that. It's like what Wayne Dyer said: "If you change the way you look at things, the things you look at will change." I had to see her for who she truly was. I made the decision to let go and move on.

She had been telling me to do so for so long and I kept fighting it. I just couldn't give up. Twenty-three years is a serious investment, but I had to cut my losses in order to truly heal and get to the next version of me.

I was wounded. My heart was cold. I never wanted to get married or have a family again. I felt betrayed, abandoned, and alone. Deep inside the real me yearned for true love. Over the years, I would fantasize about a real organic connection. An unforced natural love that was reciprocated. I told the Universe what I wanted and didn't worry about how it came to pass. I just kept working on me.

Healing is messy. One day I'm confident, I'm

up at 4 am going for a three-to-five-mile walk. I'm meditating, writing in my journal, and exercising. The next day, I can't get out of bed and I'm drowning in tears. But I kept working. I had to keep revisiting my notes from therapy and applying all that I learned. I focused on mindfulness and acceptance. I practiced a method called Cognitive Behavioral Therapy (CBT). It's based upon the idea that how you think determines how you feel and how you behave. An example is: something happens to you – you have thoughts about what just occurred – you experience emotions based upon your thoughts – you respond to your thoughts and feelings with behaviors.

The work I put into myself opened my heart again. I wasn't looking for love, but I connected with someone. I was still licking my wounds but didn't want to block my blessing and ignore the fact that this woman was perfect for me in every way and I for her. We fully vetted each other out and as a man who knows what he wants after the confirmation was planted in my head I asked her to marry me. I am now living in a fairy tale that would not be possible if I had not faced my suffering and made the hard decision to put in the work.

The greatest change comes through enduring the greatest pain. I didn't wait for the storm to pass. I locked in while surrounded by the eye of the storm and came out the other side a better man for it.

Tool: Drill
Sometimes what we need in therapy has to be slowly drilled into our minds for the shift in how we view things which will change how we make decisions.
#TamSaid

In May of 2003 I made the conscious decision to obtain a separation from my former spouse. It was a painful decision, one that I had thought about many years prior because of the uneasiness I felt with my views on life, raising children, and career aspirations. My dreams had to be in concurrence with what my former spouse wanted and just as important as her immediate family. What I learned through that process is that my perspective matters and finding a spouse that may disagree with your perspective can reach a point where they respect it. I never felt that in my prior marriage.

I decided to leave my house with the guise that the separation/divorce process would be amicable. However, it was everything but that. I left the house with a small suitcase and shortly thereafter found out I was not allowed to get personal belongings accumulated for 14 years (clothes, tools, personal effects etc.). Shortly thereafter the realities of a bitter divorce would take hold causing me to lose work opportunities, resulting in an arrest, financial problems and having to re-create my life from nothing.

Many allegations with law enforcement were leveled at me to include a trumped-up domestic violence charge that would cost me child visitation and loss of a relationship with my daughters. For a person who worked for a major law enforcement agency, I wore a scarlet letter on my back for many years. To this day, the relationship with my daughters is estranged as they have never been told my story.

During the divorce process, which lasted four years, I had to rebrand myself but in retrospect found I would unconsciously go through the stages of grief. Obviously, I had hit rock bottom and for a while lived between friends, a free apartment in a high crime neighborhood, various apartments but never shared what I was going through with family, close friends.

After stabilizing my financial situation, I was incredibly angry at women, dating a lot, not with a specific purpose but to get what I could from them. Again, on face value these women did not know what I was going through.

A few years into this, after the breakup of a relationship, I was lying in bed one night and had this talk with God about who I was. This was my *ah ha* moment when I realized my behavior was not my norm. This is where I had my breakthrough and started to self-reflect on what direction my life was going. To be honest, I do not consider myself a religious person even though I identify as Catholic and more of a spiritual persona.

I have always been a planner and because of the career damage done I decided to think of other outlets to aid in my emotional repair. One has been my commitment to fitness and teaching group fitness classes. I am certified in many group fitness formats (Cycle, Boot camp, Body Pump, Insanity, etc.). This has helped me pour out the stress of my grief and other stressors in life. Along with that I have always had an affinity for teaching, so I completed my master's degree and sought teaching opportunities. I have taught at the collegiate level now for 13 years. This afforded me another avenue to pursue post my law enforcement career and unbelievably my mentorship of students is therapeutic.

Males should not be afraid to use tools such as

therapy in which I did participate. A lesson learned from that was to give thought to your pattern of people you date. Making the same mistake repeatedly will only yield you the same results.

Lastly and the most important *ah ha* moment that night was my vow to be myself so I could be open to the possibility of a lasting relationship. God and love do work in mysterious ways as I happened to meet my current spouse in the gym. Ten years later, two wonderful children (5 and 7), retired from law enforcement, a doctorate degree, and a new career adventure. She has lovingly supported me over and beyond as I now feel my perspective matters.

If I had to give advice to males going through a divorce it would be to seek therapy outside of your family to get a varying perspective, cultivate your spirituality (I am not talking necessarily about religion), and surround yourself with supportive people that appreciate your perspectives. Throughout this journey my spouse, a few close friends, my outside activities I draw strength from, and personal spirituality have provided me with the framework to be who I am.

<u>*Tool:*</u> *The toobox*
The toolbox is necessary to keep the many tools you will need to use as you navigate the journey of divorce. Use this as a keepsake and have it readily available when you are challenged.
#TamSaid

To my Brother...
     I first want to congratulate you on taking the steps necessary to heal or help others heal. The fact that you decided to thumb through the pages of this book speaks volume. My prayer is that you find the peace you desire so you may thrive in life.

I know the hardest part may have been just that… admitting that you were hurt or dare I say *damaged*. I've witnessed many brothers over the years who fail to admit that the person they once loved and gave up so much of themselves for hurt them. He wears this mask of masculinity that allows him to show up as if he's good and has it all together until the simple mention of his ex's name or some reminder and just like that, without him even realizing, his whole demeaner changes.

Imagine the big bad strong brother, who has it all together, and at just the mention of someone's name… someone who's possibly nowhere around can possess the power to alter his mood. That's some power right there, and that my friend is one of the first steps to healing. Imagine being in a room in the middle of the summer and it's 108 degrees outside, you've had a long day and you've got the AC going. It's nice and comfortable until someone comes along unannounced and adjusts your thermostat turning of the AC.

Let's add a little spin to it. Let's say the AC is no longer just for comfort, but now it's a life-or-death necessity because there's someone near and dear that that we love with a fragile medical condition whose environment must be regulated at all times between 66-72 degrees. The game just changed, right? It's now your responsibility to make sure that one you love, the one who is near and dear to you, well-being is the priority.

You will now make sure your thermostat is protected, you will ensure that no one can alter the environment without your permission. Well bro, that person is YOU!!! And you deserve to have full control of your environment and your life. You deserve to possess and protect the emotional thermostat of your life.

How do I get back the control? Great question. I would say the first step is *Awareness…* being aware that you gave up the control of how you move through life to someone else. It's so subtle and sneaks up on you so gradually that we don't even realize it until someone else shows us. That is the toughest and biggest pill to swallow, most men (not you, of course) look at the pill in denial and kick it across the room or across the field as far and as hard as they possibly can. Come on, let's be honest here, who wants to admit that a grown man allows someone else to instantaneously alter their world, their mood, their attitude and unfortunately as I've seen in the past… initiate a moment of rage as if it was day one of the events that lead to the breakup all over again.

I was told that you can only hate someone to the degree you have the capacity to love because if you are indifferent, you cannot even get up enough energy to hate them. Again, I commend you for having the desire to get to your next level, the higher version of yourself. I challenge you to swallow this daunting pill. The good news is you have permission to chop it up or if you must, crush it up into a powder and take your time with it. No matter how you do it, just know that this proverbial "pill" has healing power that will heal you in places you didn't even realize were affected.

Assuming you're still with me and haven't closed the book after those last couple paragraphs, I'd love to share a 3-step approach that I followed. Now, it may not get you all the way to the finish line, but I guarantee you it will get you on the path to living the life you deserve. Once you've started on the path, trust and believe, you'll attract all the other needed resources that will carry you over the finish line and beyond. Ready for more? Are you wondering what's next?

Step One: **Acceptance**.

Acceptance can be tough because when we look at acceptance, the first thing that typically comes to mind is accepting fault and no one wants to accept fault, no one wants to have the guilt, or the blame of failure placed upon them. Be encouraged. I'm going to give you a different way of looking at things.

We talked about giving away power or control to someone else earlier. Now let's talk about the power of acceptance. I often ask anyone who's looking to overcome challenges in life this following question: *Can you look back over your life and take full responsibility for where you are currently?*

Sometimes it's a challenge to answer because we have the tendency of blaming others for where we are. It's easier to say it's someone else's fault that we are where we are because of what they've done to us or perhaps with us. In doing so we're looking outside at external circumstances, blaming others.

We suggest if 'so and so' didn't do this and that, my life would be different. This is a form of placing the power in someone else's hands. When others hold the power of the old past, they also hold the power to the future.

Fortunately, I often run across someone who says, "Yes! I can accept full responsibility for where I am in life." There's power in being able to accept full responsibility for where you are! That power is that you no longer have anyone else to blame, you no longer have fingers to point at anyone. The power is in knowing once you have accepted full responsibility for where you are, you also have the capability and responsibility to determine where you are headed. With that, you can choose the life you desire.

Step Two: **Forgiveness**

The "F" word is easy to say but hard to do. The danger in not forgiving often results in us drinking the poison, waiting for, and expecting the other person to die so our life can be better. All along we're consuming the poison, it's eating away at us. It's subtle, we don't even realize it until ultimately it starts to manifest in other areas of our lives.

I have an exercise that I suggest, I'll warn you now that it takes a special type of guy to do this. It's not easy, which means the rewards are worth much more than the exercise itself. Don't let simplicity negate the effects of the exercise.

> *Grab a notepad. Write out the following phrase as many times as needed. Take your time; don't feel the need to be in a rush. You may want a fresh full notepad to ensure you don't run out of paper.*

Write the following:
"Name" I forgive you for "xyz"

SAMPLE:
Kendall, I forgive you for not being there for me.
Kendall, I forgive you for not learning more about me.
Kendall, I forgive you for losing the house.
Kendall, I forgive you for the pain you've caused our family.
Kendall, I forgive you.

From the exercise, eventually you will get to the point where you'll get out all the things that you have been holding on to. And the only words left will be "*I forgive you.*" This exercise isn't for the other person, it's for you and since it's for you and only you, I'll ask you to do something else that may seem silly, unconventional, and possibly a little dangerous. Get rid of the list!!! Burn it (safely and at your own risk please), flush it down the toilet, shred it, rip it up - however you see fit. This is symbolic and for your healing.

Bruh??? Are you still with me? I realize I may lose you after this one, but that's a chance I am willing to take. I'm not here to sugar-coat my journey. It wasn't quick and quite frankly it wasn't easy; I had many "character building" days and man, I tell you it has been worth it. I've been blessed to be fully present to witness and enjoy my children growing up to become great, young adults on their way off to college to live productive lives. My adult daughter, by marriage, along with my granddaughter, and I have amazing, quality relationships, along with a host of other extended family. None of this would be possible without doing the work to heal.

I'll go out on the limb and say none of us are competing for a popularity contest. I'm sharing what has worked for me, straight, no chaser. I'm praying that you can take what we've collectively shared and use it to be a better man for yourself, your family, and your community.

Okay, we're almost done and it's okay if you aren't ready for this third and final step right now. If by chance you've made it through the prior steps, congratulations again!!! You are well on your way, and you can always come back to this exercise that will put you on another level and separate you from the crowd. Many will read these pages but only a small percentage will do the work and seriously take the necessary steps to unlock, open and walk through the doors and experience abundant life on the other side of dramatic and sometimes traumatic life.

Step Three: *Apologize*

Since you're still here I'll keep it short and sweet. By the way, I appreciate you for not tossing the book out. I'm sure the other brothers have great information that you wouldn't want to miss out on...

It's tough to apologize, especially when the apology is to the enemy or prayerfully the ex-enemy. I mentioned before that these exercises and new ways of thinking or looking at your prior experiences aren't for your ex; they are for you so you can proceed with the productive life you desire.

This apology may have to be made multiple times and it doesn't have to be perfect, deep, or long and drawn out. However, it must be done! The sooner you perform these final tasks, the sooner you can cross that finish line in the race to be healed.

How to apologize? First apologize to *yourself.* Extend some grace to yourself, show yourself some compassion, and reframe the conversations you've been having with yourself. Give yourself a new story to live by.

Second apology and I'm done... Apologize to your ex. Send a text, e-mail, send a letter, or perhaps the old-fashion way may still work. Use your voice and say the words and then move on, carry on with your life. The key here is to get it out when the time is right and **DO NOT EXPECT A RESPONSE!**

This last and final act isn't transactional, it's transformational. The transformation is for you... for us, and **NOT** for them. Don't expect anything in return and if you do get a response, cool, if not, good. I wouldn't look for or expect confirmation or anything in that realm. Detach yourself from the outcome.

Congratulations again for making it to the end of my piece and welcome to the beginning of your journey. You are now in control of your life and have the power to use it for good. Take action, do the work, pray, and take God with you every step of the way and the next time you see another brother in need share with him what worked for you. To your success…

ABOUT THE AUTHOR & VISIONARY

Meet Tamora K. Burton

Author, Speaker, Relationship & Marriage Coach, and Divorce Processing Agent, Tamora K. Burton is the author of the marriage changing book *The Marriage Policies and Procedures*. She is also the author of the bestselling devotional for divorced women who are on the road to putting the pieces back together, *Life After The "D."* Her passion lies within providing tools for couples to continue building or rebuilding the commitment necessary to sustain a thriving marriage, while being an advocate for those who have encountered the traumatic experience of divorce.

      This passion led to the successful release of two bestselling anthologies, *Life After Divorce: The Journey to Being Healed & Whole* and *Seasons of Divorce: A Reflective Journal.* Tam finds great joy in helping individuals and couples to do the work on the journey to being healed and whole. She believes that her transparency can be someone's road to recovery thus using opportunities to share her story.

Tam's greatest value add to those assigned to her purpose is offering the "missing ingredient" that she personally lacked before exchanging her very own marriage vows and finding herself divorced. After going through the journey of becoming healed and whole herself, she took the steps to date again, hence now being coined a Dating Coach. Tam's coaching style is hands-on. She has a way of delivering and teaching what dating truly is yet encouraging others to begin with dating themselves.

As she has shifted into assisting through the journey of divorce, Tam is now the Divorce Processing Agent that continues to say "yes" to those needing a personal, and spiritual view of walking through the process step by step. She is proud to launch, Life *After* Divorce, what she considers now to be a movement and not a moment. Doing the work to "Live Life Loud" is her mantra. Whether it's for a healthy relationship or marriage or locking arms with divorcees into their healing, Tam's mission is to serve.

www.tamorajohnson.net

ABOUT THE PUBLISHER & CO-SPONSOR

Meet Tanya Denise

Tanya Denise (formerly DeFreitas) is a member of the Life *After* Divorce movement. She is the publisher of this book and several of Tam's other books. Tanya's story is unique in that when she became the publisher for the women's edition, she was still married. Unfortunately, by the time the book was released, and the movement took flight, Tanya was facing divorce.

Fully submerged in the movement, in support of Tam, Tanya was surrounded by the coauthors of the women's edition who coincidently served as a support system for Tanya's new journey. As a co-sponsor of the movement's launch, Tanya's company, Writer's Block Press is also a sponsor of the men's edition.

Tanya is the Founder & Executive Director of the International Association of Women Authors (IAWA), the world's leading global network for women who write. In addition to being a certified book publisher, Tanya is a self-published, international, best-selling author, anthologist, book and writing coach. Born Latanya Hampton, in Pasadena, California, Tanya has been writing since she was a young girl, beginning her journey with poetry and short stories, then gradually growing into newsletters, newspapers, independent magazines, journals, then books.

Like Tam, Tanya is passionate about healthy relationships and marriage. An advocate for higher education,

Tanya holds a Bachelor of Science degree in Communications, with a concentration (minor) in Communication and Technology. Tanya also holds an Associate of Arts degree in Liberal Studies, and two technical education certificates, as a computerized Administrative Assistant and Accounting Clerk. She has a postbaccalaureate certificate in Marriage & Family Therapy (MFT), and another in Psychology.

Tanya's purpose is to utilize her proven faith in God to serve as a catalyst to help others heal and operate in their gift(s). Her mission is to use her gift of writing to help women and empower them to walk in their purpose. Tanya enjoys traveling, spending time with her loved ones, and trying new restaurants. She is a passionate writer, speaker, and life coach who currently makes her home in California.

For speaking engagements and or more information, please visit www.authortanyadenise.com or contact info@writersblockpress.com

There *is* **Life** ***After*** **Divorce**!